Original title:
Echoes of the Tropics

Copyright © 2025 Creative Arts Management OÜ
All rights reserved.

Author: Charles Whitfield
ISBN HARDBACK: 978-1-80581-516-7
ISBN PAPERBACK: 978-1-80581-043-8
ISBN EBOOK: 978-1-80581-516-7

Dances of the Island Spirits

In grass skirts dancing, they twist and shout,
With coconut hats that are tall and stout.
They trip over roots, oh what a sight,
As they jiggle and giggle deep into the night.

The fish join in, with fins all a-flap,
Wearing seaweed shoes in a watery nap.
Crabs play the drums on a woodpecker's log,
While the parrots laugh, it's a real carnival fog.

Harmonies of the Rain-soaked Earth

Puddles sing out in a splish-splash tune,
While frogs croak verses beneath the moon.
Worms waltz on the stage, soft and squishy,
While the clouds above look a bit too mushy.

Raindrops tap dance on banana leaves,
Each splash a new joke that the stillness weaves.
The sun peeks out, takes the stage for a laugh,
Then slips behind clouds, like it's shy from the staff.

Ripening Dreams Beneath the Tropics

Mangoes tumble from trees, giving chase,
While the parrots squawk, 'This is our space!'
Coconuts roll like they're in a race,
Hoping to win with a smile on their face.

The bananas gossip, swinging side to side,
'Did you hear about Jack who got stuck in a ride?'
The laughter erupts as the fruit gets ripe,
In a world filled with silliness, fun is the hype.

The Voice of the Swaying Palms

The palms whisper secrets in the breeze,
'Watch out for monkeys, they're sneaky with ease!'
They shake their fronds, holding back a grin,
As a goat tries to climb, thinking it's thin.

They sway and chuckle, oh what a show,
As kids run in circles, yelling, 'Let's go!'
With sand in their toes and joy all around,
These cheeky old palms are the life of the ground.

Vows Beneath the Tropical Stars

Under stars that twinkle bright,
We promised not to start a fight.
But then a crab stole our food,
And suddenly, we were in the mood.

With coconut drinks in hand,
We swore to form a reggae band.
But when we strummed that first note,
Even the fish jumped from the boat!

Amid the palms that danced and swayed,
Our vows got lost in the parade.
The monkeys laughed, the parrots squawked,
While we just sat there, dumbstruck, shocked!

So here's to love beneath the moon,
And to our latest off-key tune.
For every vow that's made in jest,
In this wild place, we love the best!

Lament of the Sun-Drenched Shore

Oh, the sun shines bright, oh what a pain,
The sand's so hot, it could drive us insane.
We tried to build a castle of dreams,
But seagulls swooped in like food-fueled schemes.

A crab pinched my toe, I yelped in fright,
While my friend fell asleep, a comical sight.
The waves kept crashing, a continuous roar,
And we just laughed on that sunny shore.

With sunscreen smeared, we looked quite absurd,
Like walking fries, or so I heard.
But every laugh, every bruise we earned,
Gives us stories that we never spurned.

So raise your cups to the silly, the fun,
In the glow of the day, or when day is done.
Forever we'll joke 'bout the heat and the sand,
Life's a big giggle in this tropical land!

Secrets of the Lush Wilderness

In the jungle, a monkey swings,
He drops his lunch—oh, what a fling!
A parrot squawks, "Pick it up, dude!"
He shrugs, "I was hungry, not rude!"

Vines twist round a dancer's feet,
She dances high, then lands on a beet!
The beetle squeaks, "Hey, watch your tread!"
She laughs, "Sorry, I just love this spread!"

Voices from the Island Shore

Crabs in tuxedos prance on the sand,
"More pinching, less walking!" is their band.
A fish jumps high, says, "Join the fun!"
"Just don't splash! I'm all dressed for sun!"

Seagulls argue over lunchtime fries,
"That's my share!"—then one quickly flies.
A beach ball rolls and hits a palm,
"Sorry, guys! This game's quite the charm!"

Tides of Swaying Sorrows

A sea turtle ponders life on the wave,
"Why go slow when I can misbehave?"
He rides a swell, with a cheeky grin,
"C'mon, friends! Let the fun begin!"

The dolphins flip in synchronized dance,
Their funny twirls invite a glance.
A fish yells, "Hey, no time for tears!"
"Just laughs and splashes, let's conquer fears!"

Mists Over Verdant Valleys

A sloth climbs high, but it's quite a task,
"Why run fast? I prefer to bask!"
The clouds giggle, as if they know,
He just found out he's too slow to show.

Frogs wear hats, holding tiny tea,
"Join our party, or just hop with glee!"
A breeze whispers, "Dance like the leaves!"
"But we're frogs, not dancers!" one of them grieves.

Songs Carried by the Ocean Winds

A crab donned a hat, oh so bright,
Danced on the sand in pure delight.
Whales sang to fish, a funny tune,
Seaweed clapped under the sun and moon.

Seagulls squawked, a raucous choir,
Pirates joined in, their voices higher.
With coconut drums they made quite a show,
While fish in tuxedos swam to and fro.

Flickers of Fireflies at Dusk

Fireflies blinked like starlit eyes,
Danced on the breeze, much to our surprise.
A frog in a top hat sang a ballad,
While crickets played tunes that were quite valid.

They twinkled and winked, a twirling spree,
A glowing parade, what fun to see!
A firefly grinned, 'This is the life!'
While the moths all buzzed, 'We'll avoid the strife!'

The Heartbeat of the Jungle

A monkey forgot how to swing just right,
Tumbled down from a branch, oh what a sight!
Parrots chuckled, in colors so bold,
While the jaguar yawned, feeling quite old.

Vines played tag, much stronger than it seems,
Lions whispered, 'Shall we chase our dreams?'
A sloth took a nap, declaring with glee,
"I'm winning this race, just wait and see!"

Murmurs of the Native Lands

The wind carried tales of silly goats,
Who wore tiny boots and rarely wrote notes.
Rattlesnakes rattled their own beats,
While rabbits served tea, offering sweets.

A wise old turtle whispered, 'Take care,'
As the squirrels rehearsed a daring air fair.
With laughter and cheer, under the sun's rays,
They danced in the fields, counting the days.

Breezes that Kiss the Skies

The wind whispers jokes to the palm,
While coconuts chuckle, staying calm.
Parrots squawk laughter, full of cheer,
As the sun tickles the atmosphere.

Flip-flops dance on sandy floors,
Crabs in tuxedos, opening doors.
The sun is a comedian, bright and bold,
Jokes of the tropics never grow old.

The Lure of Lush Greenery

Plants wear hats made of rain and sun,
Each leaf a grin, oh what fun!
Vines swing wildly, they take a trip,
While flowers giggle, in a floral whip.

Monkeys throw fruit, a fruity surprise,
With each flying banana, laughter flies.
The jungle sings with a playful tune,
As frogs croak songs to the glowing moon.

Currents of the Moonlit Sea

Waves wave fondly, a splashy tease,
Fish dress in glitter, swim with ease.
Starfish applaud with limbs spread wide,
While mermaids laugh, a joyride glide.

The moon's a jokester, casting its light,
Tickling the waves, oh what a sight!
Surfboards giggle, taking a leap,
While dolphins prank, losing their sleep.

Blossoms Beneath the Canopy

Under the roof of a leafy dome,
Flowers tell stories, far from home.
Bees buzz jokes, a sweet, funny hum,
As butterflies dance to the rhythm of drum.

The forest whispers, secrets to share,
With laughter echoing through the air.
Toadstools giggle, in hues so bright,
In this playful world, all feels just right.

Traces of Serenity in Bloom

In the garden, butterflies dance,
Wearing socks around their pants,
They sip tea with a butterfly's grace,
While lilies giggle in their place.

Sunflowers yawning at the dawn,
Crickets play their early song,
The breeze whispers a silly tune,
As the moon starts to munch on a prune.

Bees in hats buzz by the hive,
Declaring boldly they thrive live,
Ladybugs race on tiny cars,
Chasing dreams under candy bars.

When the sun sets with a wink,
Trees start to giggle, make you think,
Silly shadows stretching wide,
Chasing fireflies, they laugh and glide.

Flickers of Color in a Sunbeam

Parrots juggling in the air,
Spinning circles without a care,
While munching snacks of golden fries,
With surprise cakes, they aim for the skies.

Sunbeams tickle a playful lizard,
Wristwatch turtles taking a gizzard,
They moonwalk on the sandy shore,
While crabs do backflips, asking for more.

Watermelons lounging with flair,
Sipping punch in their fruity lair,
Coconuts sing a joyous song,
While pineapples cheer them all along.

As dusk wraps the sky in pink,
Laughter spills over the drink,
Stars in little hats peek out,
Joining in the fun without a doubt.

Legend of the Twilight Oasis

In the twilight, camels wear ties,
Sipping smoothies, oh what a surprise,
With sunglasses perched on their snouts,
They gossip about the pouts of trout.

Cacti do the cha-cha at night,
Under stars that twinkle so bright,
With tumbleweeds bouncing around,
While the night owl plays the merry-go-round.

Lizards strumming guitars so sweet,
Dancing to the rattlesnake beat,
As toads join in with a croak and a cheer,
Creating a band that you'd want to hear.

When the moon lights up the sand,
Everyone joins in, hand in hand,
In the oasis, the fun won't cease,
Legends are born, and laughter's the lease.

Dreams Wrapped in Hibiscus

In the garden of bright delight,
Hibiscus dream of silly sights,
With flavors like candy in the air,
Lemons giggle without a care.

Rainbow lizards in socks so bold,
Tell stories of treasures untold,
As butterflies paint the skies so wide,
While jammin' frogs hop side by side.

Sunset parties on the lawn,
With giggles shared until the dawn,
Tropical drinks in cups of stars,
As coconut crabs rock-out on guitars.

When the dawn bursts with laughter bright,
Flowers dance with pure delight,
In every petal, a secret to find,
Wrapped in joy, forever aligned.

Whispers of the Rainforest

In the jungle, a parrot squawks,
He thinks he's clever, but just mocks.
A monkey swings, can't find his hat,
Turns around, thinks he's a cool cat.

A sloth hangs upside down, so slow,
Takes an hour just to say hello.
The toucan's beak, so bright and long,
Sings off-key, thinks he's in a song.

In the bushes, a frog tries to sing,
Sounds like a rubber band, that's his thing.
A snake takes a nap, dreams of a mouse,
But dreams won't save him from an owl's house.

Laughter dances through leafy lanes,
In this place where whimsy reigns.
Nature's circus, what a delight,
Join the fun from morning till night.

Songs of the Vibrant Canopy

The tree frogs croak a tuneful tune,
Their rhythm makes the stars swoon.
A squirrel juggles acorns with flair,
While a sloth is caught in a slow dance affair.

An iguana basking high and proud,
Claims he's the king over this crowd.
But below him, the ants march in line,
Doing the cha-cha, oh how divine!

A toucan sports a silly hat,
In a fashion show with another chitchat.
The sound of laughter fills the air,
And all the critters dance without a care!

In canopies where giggles blend,
Life's a joke that has no end.
Join the revelry, take a chance,
The forest sways, let's sing and dance!

Murmurs Beneath the Palms

Under palms, where crickets hum,
A beetle plays a tiny drum.
Chatter from the lizards above,
Confesses secrets of jungle love.

The breeze carries whispers of jest,
As the flamingos pose, all dressed.
A capybara lounges, steals the scene,
With a smile that's remarkably keen.

A palm tree leans as if to hear,
A gossiping monkey who draws near.
A parrot's tale, a tad absurd,
"Did you hear what the peacock heard?"

Amidst the shade, laughter flows,
In this wild world, anything goes.
Join the fun in the sunshine's beam,
Where every moment is a crazy dream!

Shadows of the Sunlit Jungle

Beneath the sun, shadows start to tease,
A raccoon's scheming for some cheese.
Chasing butterflies, he trips on air,
And lands with a thud, not a single care.

A jaguar yawns, a sleepy sight,
Wishing for naps instead of fights.
While a toucan's trying to catch a line,
But all that comes out is a funny whine.

Lizards play leapfrog, quick as a flash,
While sloths cheer on, a slow-motion clash.
In this merry game of the day,
Everyone's looking to laugh and play!

The jungle's alive with playful glee,
In every nook, there's fun to see.
With sunlit hues, join the parade,
Where shadows dance and mischief's made!

Elysium in the Mist

In the haze, a monkey swings,
Chasing dreams with silly flings.
Coconuts fall, then bounce away,
As giggles fill the bright, warm day.

A parrot squawks, it's quite absurd,
It mispronounces every word.
Sipping rum from a painted shell,
Laughing hard, oh, what a spell!

Wet hammocks sway, the breeze is cheeky,
As tourists dance, a bit too freaky.
Sunburned backs, in stripes of red,
Hot beach chairs serve as cozy bed.

A crab in shades, struts with delight,
Doing the cha-cha, such a sight.
In this place where giggles sprout,
Life's a fest, without a doubt.

The Soul of Island Serenity

Palm trees sway with rhythmic grace,
A lizard sneezes, what a case!
A hammock holds a snoozing chap,
Who dreams of fish in sunny clap.

Three turtles race, or so they claim,
But slowly shuffle, what a game!
A crab with swagger walks on by,
No hurry here, just chill and sigh.

In the shade, a loud old parrot,
Sings of love for some old carrot.
The sun sets low, all painted gold,
With laughter shared, the best stories told.

A tie-dye shirt spins in the breeze,
Falling off a dancing knees.
In this realm of calm delight,
Every day feels just so right.

Tempos of the Changing Winds

In the wind, a kite takes flight,
Tangled in the palm tree's might.
Children laugh as it flops down,
A battle lost, they look like clowns.

A dolphin leaps in cheeky spins,
While tourists cheer for its wild wins.
But one slips on a fishy snack,
And lands in waves with quite a smack.

The great big sun wears shades of pink,
As island charm makes faces wink.
Surfboards tumble in joyous sway,
Riding waves, life's one big play.

With every gust, new antics come,
It's fun around, so let's not glum.
In this wild, tropical domain,
Every challenge sounds like a game.

Vibrant Life's Resonant Glee

On the shore, where laughter roams,
A poodle swims, as if it's homes!
With floaties on, it's quite the sight,
A regal dog in ocean's bite.

Bamboo sticks hold fishy treats,
While crabs join in for tasty feats.
The beach is full of silly sounds,
As rhythm dances all around.

Coconuts roll, like bouncy balls,
As islanders answer playful calls.
One trip and tumble in the sand,
This paradise, so strange and grand.

Seaweed hats atop young heads,
With giggles shared from sunlit beds.
In vibrant hues, the day unfolds,
Each moment shines, a tale retold.

Echoing Colors of the Paradisiacal

In a land where parrots squawk,
Silly monkeys talk like hawks.
Palm trees wave with breezy flair,
They dance around without a care.

Bright colors paint the vibrant sky,
While fishes leap and dolphins fly.
Sandals stuck in melting sand,
Oh, this joy is quite unplanned!

The sun sneezes, rays spread wide,
People slip on sunblock, glide.
Coconuts fall like ancient stones,
Laughter echoes, silly tones.

Beneath the palms, the tourists grin,
Chasing crabs that scuttle in.
With every laugh, a tropical twist,
In this paradise, you can't resist!

Romantic Hues of Tropical Dreams

Coconut drinks and flamingo cheeks,
Embarrassed blush, where laughter peaks.
Under stars, couples often sway,
While jellyfish dance in the bay.

Moonlight kisses the ocean's wave,
Forgotten vows are hard to save.
Romance blooms with a crabby twist,
Bumping heads in an awkward kiss!

With ukulele strumming near,
Lovebirds whisper, oh so dear.
While a parrot shouts, 'Hey there, mates!'
Love's drowned out by feathered mates!

Tropical nights weave rich delight,
With swaying hips that feel so right.
In the midst of love's wild scheme,
We trip on sandals in this dream!

Puzzles Beneath the Foliage

In thick green leaves, the secrets lie,
But squirrels gossip while birds fly.
Puzzles scattered, a treasure hunt,
Lost flip-flops and a coconut stunt!

Frogs croak riddles in the rain,
With quirky hats, they'd drive you insane.
The ground's alive with playful fuss,
Who'd guess they'd ride a patterned bus?

A sloth hangs low, plays peek-a-boo,
While tourists step on a loafer shoe.
The hidden trails twist and bend,
Boys chase after... where does that end?

Ants march in a silly line,
'We're on a quest, so feel divine!'
Beneath the foliage, laughter wakes,
In these puzzles, joy overtakes!

The Lure of the Ocean's Embrace

Waves play tag with toes and feet,
Shells whisper, hearts skip a beat.
A beach ball zooms, a giggly toss,
Sunburnt noses, oh, what a loss!

Sandcastles rise, but all fall down,
As children laugh, while parents frown.
A crab steals snacks from clever hands,
Mom waves a shoe; it's war, on sands!

The tide pulls back, with playful tease,
Bringing fishes who aim to please.
Oh, watch the flips of a playful seal,
In warm waters where joy feels real.

Surfboards tumble, griping knuckles,
Someone's fallen, hear the chuckles!
With ocean's call, we chase the sun,
In this embrace, we all have fun!

Landscape of Exotic Whispers

In the jungle, parrots squawk,
They gossip like they're on a walk.
A monkey steals my picnic lunch,
It grins at me, a cheeky hunch.

The trees wear hats of vibrant green,
They shimmy like they've just been seen.
A sloth thinks he's a racing car,
But moves like syrup from a jar.

Down by the river, fish that dance,
With fins that wave, they take their chance.
A turtle winks, then strikes a pose,
"I'm fast," it claims, "but who really knows?"

Amid the blooms where laughter grows,
A bee makes jokes nobody knows.
The air is sweet, like candy floss,
In this wild world, we're all at loss.

The Heartbeat of Teeming Life

Beneath the sun, the critters crawl,
A lizard slips; what a great fall!
A chameleon wears all the hues,
Fashion sense? It's got the clues.

The ants throw parties, small and grand,
With tiny snacks, they feast and stand.
A cricket plays a tune so bright,
While fireflies dance, it's quite a sight.

Frogs croak jokes that make them laugh,
While turtles ponder their own path.
The world spins round, a circus show,
With every creature in the flow.

When night falls, the moon takes flight,
And stars join in, a sparkly sight.
Together they hum a silly tune,
All creatures grooving 'neath the moon.

Visions of Swaying Grass

The grass stands tall, an emerald sea,
It tickles noses, oh how free!
A rabbit hops with flair and grace,
While a turtle takes its time, slow pace.

A breeze arrives, it plays a game,
The flowers dance, but feel no shame.
A butterfly wears polka dots,
It flits and flutters, tying knots.

In this patchwork tapestry bright,
Bees zoom around, they're quite a sight.
Grasshoppers leap, they have a blast,
While crickets chirp, their shadows cast.

The sun dips low, a golden orb,
As night brings tales that we absorb.
The grass whispers secrets we can't hear,
Of silly dreams held very dear.

Rhumba of the Rolling Waves

The waves crash down with a funny grin,
Each one has tales of where it's been.
A dolphin spins, it takes a dive,
With flips and flips, it feels alive.

Seagulls squawk in a melodious way,
"Join the dance," they seem to say.
A crab jives sideways, a dance so grand,
While starfish winks, "Aren't we fanned?"

The sun sets low, the sky ablaze,
On the shore, we wander in a daze.
Sand castles rise, but then they fall,
The waves giggle, "Come join us, all!"

As night unfolds, the rhythm flows,
Moonlight joins in, and the fun grows.
The ocean hums a playful tune,
Where laughter echoes, and hearts are strewn.

Pulses of Lush Serenity

In a jungle where fruit sings,
Monkeys dance on rubber bands,
Claiming every ripe offering,
While parakeets throw up their hands.

A sloth moves with utmost flair,
While turtles sprint with wild need,
The laughter brewed in the thick air,
As the iguanas paint and bead.

Coconuts drop with comic plops,
And the toucans squawk like glee,
As the party never stops,
In this world, oh so carefree.

There's a parrot that tells jokes,
With a beak full of wit and sass,
Cracking up all the fine folks,
In this jungle's merry mass.

Breaths of the Infinite Sky

Up above, the clouds do giggle,
Like fluffy marshmallows they sway,
While a crow plays the fiddle,
Trying to steal the day.

Dancing with the zephyr's breeze,
The kites are tangled with pure joy,
As the sun turns into cheese,
For every girl and boy.

Frogs croak choruses of cheer,
While the owls hoot in delight,
Winking at those passing near,
In a festival of light.

With every glinting star's arrival,
The night wears its shimmering gown,
Laughter's the universal survival,
In the sky's glorious crown.

Tides of Ancient Stories

The waves dance with tales of yore,
In a language of sloshing bliss,
Seashells whisper from the shore,
A symphony you can't miss.

An octopus holds court with flair,
While crabs conspire in disguise,
With a wink and little scare,
Catching fish with clever lies.

Starfish giggle, sandcastles grow,
As tides retreat with a sneaky grin,
In a land where the fun must flow,
And the mermaids join right in.

The ocean's tales, forever spun,
Make seagulls chuckle in the sun,
With surfboards made of wishes won,
The beach is always just as fun.

Vivid Life in a Sunlit Realm

In a garden brimming with cheer,
Flowers wear hats just for fun,
Butterflies buzzing so near,
Chasing after the golden sun.

Ants parade with tiny pluck,
As ladybugs roll on the ground,
They've found their stride and their luck,
In a world so joyfully abound.

A sunbeam tickles the warm leaves,
While frogs wear crowns in the mud,
Each moment's a jest that believes,
In the humor of nature's flood.

Every laugh in this vivid scene,
Makes the day glow with delight,
In a realm where all's serene,
And every heart finds its light.

Voices in the Twilight Mist

In the jungle, monkeys swing,
Chasing dreams and butterflies.
A parrot tells a silly joke,
While crickets compete for the prize.

Lizards dance on a flat, wet rock,
With a beat that makes them sway.
Raccoons band together to sing,
Though a cat steals the show and plays.

At dusk, fireflies twinkle bright,
Like tiny lamps in the gloom.
They flash a message: 'Party here!'
While the frogs croak, "Make room!"

The night falls, laughter's afloat,
A symphony of silly sounds.
Tropical fun in every note,
As nature's zest knows no bounds.

Resonance of the Coconut Grove

In a grove where coconuts fall,
A squirrel claims a prize for flair.
He flips, he spins, then makes a call,
While waiting for a curious bear.

Turtles take their sweet, old time,
Playing cards under palm shade.
As dolphins judge their rhythm rhyme,
Their skills in samba displayed.

Parrots squawk with witty charm,
Trading puns with great delight.
A crab attempts a two-step arm,
But adds a slip, it's quite the sight!

As twilight gathers, fun begins,
A history of mischief grows.
In this grove where laughter spins,
The fun is where the wild wind blows.

Lullabies of the Cinnamon Isles

In the breeze, spices sing sweet,
While a seagull preens its wing.
The waves clap their hands to their beat,
And driftwood dances in a swing.

Bananas wear a peel of pride,
As coconuts cheerfully roll.
While fish in costumes take a ride,
Dressed to steal the ocean's soul.

On sandy shores, a crab takes naps,
With a beach hat that just won't stay.
Turtles exchange their fancy maps,
Of secrets found at the bay.

The moon rises, a stage is set,
For everyone to show their skills.
And as the stars begin to fret,
It's the night of giggles and thrills.

Rhythms of the Tropical Night

When night comes, the moon starts to sway,
As bats join in a wild chase.
A lizard struts like it's Broadway,
And crickets hop with perfect grace.

Fireflies flash and start a dance,
A limbo under the starlit glow.
Each pinata waits for its chance,
Sweet pinwheel dreams are all aglow.

A toucan beats a bongo drum,
While iguanas break-fall to cheer.
A turtle's back makes a good hum,
As nature joins the fun all year.

As laughter rings and shadows play,
The night is cheerful and bright.
Under the stars, join the ballet,
The rhythms of pure delight!

Hums of the Exotic Breeze

In the jungle, monkeys swing,
A fruit salad, they do bring.
Chasing birds with silly glee,
Trumpeting their melody.

Lizards sunbathe, oh so proud,
Dancing under laughter loud.
A breeze that tickles tree and leaf,
Nature's jesters, oh so brief.

Chants of the Lush Green

Frogs in chorus, croaks in tune,
Hopping underneath the moon.
Parrots squawking, vibrant cheer,
Can you hear? Oh yes, they're near!

Giant ferns with silly hats,
A dance-off with the acrobats.
In the shade, all creatures prance,
Join the game, let's take a chance!

Secrets of the Coral Reef

Fish wear sweaters, quite absurd,
Wiggling tails without a word.
Octopuses play hide and seek,
Bubbles rise, their laughter cheek!

Turtles race with utmost grace,
But trip on algae, oh what a face!
Starfish giggle in their spots,
Raising arms, they've tied their knots.

Refrains of the Sensuous Shore

Crabs in tuxedos scuttle fast,
Waving claws, a beachside blast.
Seagulls dive for chips galore,
Only to find they want much more!

Sunbathers snooze, hats on their heads,
Dreaming of tropical bred spreads.
Waves that tickle toes, they roar,
Joyful antics, who could ask for more?

Ballad of Hidden Waterfalls

In the jungle where monkeys swing,
A waterfall hides, oh, what a thing!
Splashing water, a slippery dance,
Even the frogs are caught in a trance.

Fish in raincoats, they swim with style,
While the crabs compete for the best smile.
A parrot jokes with a cheeky squawk,
"Don't slip on a rock, it's a whole wet walk!"

Mushrooms giggle from the dampened ground,
While the wet dog shakes, spins all around.
Each drop of water, a secret giggle,
Nature's humor in every wiggle.

So come to see this watery play,
Where laughter bubbles in a silly spray.
The secret here is not just the show,
It's joy that flows wherever you go!

Chronicles of Colorful Flora

Petals bright with shades galore,
Dancing bees knock on the door.
"Come in! We've got pollen to share!"
Said the rose with a flair beyond compare.

Dandelions wish to be like a star,
While grasshoppers claim they can leap far.
In this garden, humor blooms wide,
With sunflowers laughing, full of pride.

Lizards strut, a fashion parade,
In leaves so green, they've got it made.
But one fell down, oh what a scene,
He wiggled his tail—an impromptu routine!

So join the fiesta of color and cheer,
Each petal a wink, all want you near.
A garden party, nature's delight,
Blooming antics from morning till night!

Fantasies in the Canopy

High in the trees, where the parrots play,
A sloth yawns loud, "Is it the end of the day?"
His slow-motion moves are quite the treat,
He'll dance for you—if you have a seat!

Baboons are gossiping, swinging their tails,
While squirrels recount their latest tales.
"Did you see the owl?" one cheekily grins,
"His hoots have more style than our closest wins!"

The leaves rustle with a ticklish breeze,
As vines tickle cheeks like the greatest tease.
A raccoon sneezes, "Oops, pardon me!"
As butterflies laugh, filled with glee.

So if you climb this leafy spree,
Expect giggles from branches and glee from the trees.
In this world above, where laughter is free,
There's always a surprise waiting for thee!

Tides of Whispering Waves

Waves crash in a back-and-forth jig,
Fish flaunt their fins like they're doing a gig.
A turtle shouts, 'Catch me if you can!'
While the seaweed sways to its watery plan.

Crabs in a race, with shells that gleam,
They scuttle and scramble, it's quite the theme.
"I'm winning!" one shouts, then trips on a shell,
Rolling away while the others yell.

Seagulls dive with a cheeky sweep,
While the sun casts shadows on waves that leap.
A surfboard tumbles, a splash in the air,
As laughter rides the tides everywhere.

So come to the shore where the fun never ends,
With each splash and giggle, the ocean befriends.
In this watery world, let your worries all fade,
Where joy runs rampant, and laughter's not delayed!

Footprints on the Sandy Symphonies

Footprints dance on golden sands,
As crabs wave with tiny hands.
Laughter bubbles, seashells sing,
Each wave a mischievous fling.

A parrot squawks a cheeky joke,
While sunburned tourists want to smoke.
A beach ball flies, oh what a sight!
Chasing each other, pure delight.

Sandcastles rise, then swiftly fall,
Brave knights from wet, dethroned halls.
Here comes a wave! Oh no, oh dear!
The sandy throne has disappeared!

Under the sun, we never stop,
With ice cream drips, it's a sticky flop.
But laughter soars like kites in flight,
In these sandy symphonies, life's just right.

Light Filtering Through the Leaves

Sunbeams peek through a leafy hat,
Dancing bakeries of sunlit chat.
Monkeys giggle, swinging high,
While butterflies flutter by, oh my!

Coconuts drop with a pitter-pat,
Shells become hats, imagine that!
Frogs croak songs in perfect sound,
Where every leaf is humor-bound.

Laughter ripples through vibrant vines,
As the world winks, and sunshine shines.
A squirrel drops a nut on a toe,
Nature's giggles in the flow.

With each rustling, a secret's shared,
In the canopy, no one's spared.
The light breaks through, a playful dance,
Nature's jest, life's sweet chance.

Tales Woven in Foliage

In the thicket, stories bloom,
A chameleon paints its room.
Frogs in top hats, they parade,
In leafy halls where mischief's made.

Lizards tell tales, long and tall,
About the times they teetered and fell.
Vines entwine in most humorous knots,
Whispering secrets, weaving plots.

A sloth plays chess with a bright green snake,
That moves so slowly, it's hard to take.
In wild banter, the fables grow,
Where leaves and laughter intertwine in flow.

As the sun dips, shadows grow bold,
The foliage giggles, stories unfold.
In this playful realm of the wise,
Nature's humor always flies high.

The Pulse of the Tropical Dawn

A rooster crows with morning cheer,
Raising eyebrows and cups of beer.
As the sun yawns, the day begins,
With whispers of mischief and playful spins.

Waves rustle secrets on the shore,
While palm trees sway, wanting more.
Coffee brews with a mischievous twist,
As sleepyheads can't help but tryst.

A toucan winks with a vibrant beak,
Chasing the clouds with a cheeky squeak.
In the dawn's blush, a shy iguana waits,
For the man's hat – he's plotting fates!

Tropical rhythms in every beat,
As laughter compounds with every treat.
The day unfolds with joyful glee,
In nature's pulse, we dance carefree.

Fables of the Breathing Wilderness

In the jungle, a parrot spoke,
To a monkey, who thought it a joke.
They played tag with a giant snail,
But that sneaky guy left a slimy trail.

The sloth, in his slow-motion race,
Declared he'd win without any pace.
The iguana rolled his bright eyes,
While a toucan cawed, 'Oh, what a surprise!'

A capybara strutted, quite proud,
Trying to dance in front of the crowd.
With a belly flop, he fell headlong,
The fish splashed him; they sang their song.

Thus, in a realm of joy and jest,
Nature resumes her playful quest.
Each creature laughs, under wide skies,
In the tapestry of fun that never dies.

The Dance of Sun and Shadow

The sun donned shades, looking quite cool,
While the shadow made a splash in the pool.
They waltzed around, a quirky pair,
Strutting their stuff without a care.

A palm tree sighed as it watched their show,
With a breeze that whispered, 'Take it slow!'
But the sun was bright, and the shadow long,
Creating a dance that felt like a song.

A crab tapped its claws on the sand,
Joining the rhythm, all unplanned.
A stray dog chased after a kite,
While the sun giggled, oh what a sight!

Laughter echoed through vibrant greens,
In this dance where nothing's as it seems.
Sun and shadow, a comedic sight,
Under the laughter of the golden light.

A Symphony of Ephemeral Skies

Clouds gathered for a talent show,
Each one flaunting a breezy flow.
One tried to float, but dropped a rain,
The audience gasped; it was quite the gain!

A lightning bolt played a saxophone,
While thunder joined in, deep and grown.
The sun burst in, a diva's delight,
Singing a tune that was brilliantly bright.

A flock of birds joined with a cheer,
Turning the chaos to a clear sheer.
They squawked and danced, in a joyful haze,
Creating a melody that could amaze.

Thus, beneath the vast dome of blue,
Nature's stage put on quite the view.
With giggles and blunders, moments collide,
In a wild concert where joys abide.

Tapestry of Tropical Twilight

The fireflies blinked, like tiny stars,
Inviting the frogs to join in their cars.
A cricket serenaded the night,
As lizards strutted, feeling alright.

In the dusk, shadows began to peep,
Chasing their dreams as the world fell asleep.
A slumbering iguana let out a yawn,
While the moon laughed, saying, 'Come on, come on!'

The stars played hide and seek with the trees,
Turning the night into a breeze.
As the nocturnal band took their cue,
A symphony rang out, the fun was due!

Such frolic in twilight's embrace,
Every creature finds its place.
With giggles and chirps, the night unfolds,
In a lively world where fun is bold.

Serenades of the Mango Orchard

In the grove, the mangoes dance,
Sway with rhythm, give chance a glance.
Parrots squawk and monkeys swing,
Who knew fruit could do such a thing?

With each bite, a juice spree's begun,
Sticky hands, oh, what a fun run!
Underneath the sun's bright grin,
Mango pit fights, let the games begin!

Laughter rises, oh what a show,
Sunshine cheer, our colorful glow.
A pit rolls this way, dodged with glee,
Tell the bitter uncle, "Not for thee!"

Every tree has stories to tell,
Of sweet fruit naps and a sticky spell.
In the orchard, joy does not hide,
With laughing friends, it's a wild ride!

Cadence of the Rainfall

Pitter-patter on the rooftop's tune,
Dancing raindrops beneath the moon.
Umbrellas open like flowers in bloom,
As puddles form, we twirl and zoom!

Splish and splash in joyful delight,
Who knew rain could be such a fright?
Slipping and sliding, a comical sight,
With squishy socks, time feels just right!

A thunder's joke rolls through the air,
Laughing clouds, they simply don't care.
Bouncing off the streets like a ball,
In this wet dance, we're having a ball!

All around, laughter fizzes and pops,
As rain falls down, the fun never stops.
We'll catch every drop for a taste of sweet cheer,
In the cadence of rain, there's nothing to fear!

Lappings of the Ocean Tide

Waves come in with a playful grin,
Tickling toes, let the games begin!
Sandcastles high, topped with seaweed,
Who knew a beach could be so freed?

A crab scuttles with a sideways dance,
While seagulls squawk at mischance.
Flip-flops flying, lost in the spree,
As we chase our dreams by the salty sea!

Splashing and laughing, we roll with the waves,
Ocean's laughter, oh how it paves!
Dolphins leap, in a jubilant arc,
As we gather shells, spontaneously sparked!

Tide pools giggle, holding secrets inside,
With fishy friends, we drift and glide.
In this watery world of silly and bright,
We share our smiles till the fall of night!

Hues of the Dusking Horizon

Sunset paints skies with colors so bold,
As day bids goodnight, tired stories unfold.
Fireflies flicker a welcome-back dance,
Nature's stage sets with a glow, a chance!

Laughter echoes with the crickets' tune,
Underneath the watchful moon.
Stars tickle twinkles in pure delight,
As we share silly tales of nighttime fright!

Marshmallows roast on sticks that are bent,
S'mores in hand, laughter's the main event.
The sky is a canvas, our smiles the paint,
As we weave memories without restraint!

One by one, the stars take their place,
A dazzling night in this joyful space.
With giggles and grins, we beckon the night,
In hues of laughter, everything feels right!

Melodies at Dusk's Door

A monkey swings with glee,
His laughter fills the air,
He juggles juicy fruits,
While we all stop and stare.

The iguana hums a tune,
In shades of green so bright,
A parrot joins the chorus,
With feathers catching light.

A breeze that tickles noses,
As slippers take a flight,
A dance between the palm trees,
What a silly sight!

And when the sun is sinking,
The crickets sing their song,
With rhythms so contagious,
You can't help but dance along!

Vibrations of the Parrot's Call

A parrot wears a top hat,
With sunglasses on his beak,
He talks of life's great wonders,
In a voice so very cheek!

He tells the best of stories,
Of fruits and tasty pies,
While monkeys cheer his jokes,
'Cause laughter never dies.

The toucan sneezes loudly,
And drops his berry treat,
The jungle shakes with laughter,
From this unexpected feat!

Underneath the palm leaves,
Where palm wine flows like streams,
A party grows with feathers,
And everyone just beams!

Skylines of Verdant Splendor

The sun peeks through the branches,
With rays that tickle toes,
A sloth is dancing sideways,
In moves we can't suppose!

A turtle in a bow tie,
Struts proudly on the trail,
While frogs conduct a symphony,
And frogs jump without fail.

The butterflies hold concerts,
With wings that flap in time,
Each note a gentle giggle,
In colors bright and prime!

A squirrel plays the maracas,
With acorns for a beat,
This band of jungle creatures,
Makes rhythms oh so sweet!

Ripples on the Surface of Delight

A dolphin jumps with laughter,
As fish dance in their schools,
While turtles tease the seagulls,
About their slow-paced rules!

The crabs are on a mission,
Of secrets deep beneath,
They whisper to the starfish,
While playing tricks with reefs.

A pelican in laughter,
Attempts to catch a breeze,
But finds himself in awkward,
Splashing 'round like he's at ease!

Oh, what a sight of humor,
In waters cool and bright,
Where every splash is joyful,
Beneath the moon's warm light!

Echoes in the Canopy

A parrot wearing shades, oh what a sight,
Sipping on coconuts, feeling quite bright.
Monkeys in shorts swing, strut with great flair,
They laugh at the sloths, who just sit and stare.

A toucan on a branch plays hide-and-seek,
With lumbering iguanas, oh isn't that peak?
Laughter rings loudly through the leafy maze,
While frogs tell jokes that leave all amazed.

Bamboo trumpets sound, a tropical band,
Playing tunes so funky, they make you dance unplanned.
Even the palms sway, giggling in time,
As the sun winks down, in its glow so sublime.

Underneath the vibrant, swaying green shade,
Creatures gather 'round, each mimicking the trade.
They throw a big party, with snacks from the trees,
Where laughter is loud, and worries cease to please.

Reflections on the Amber Waters

On golden shores where waves tickle toes,
Crabs wear tiny hats, striking funny poses.
Fish in their schools, with patterns so bright,
One tried a ballet, but slipped—oh what a sight!

A dolphin on a surfboard, catching a wave,
Cracks jokes with the tourists, oh how they rave!
While seagulls circle, with chips in their beaks,
Cheeky little thieves, they play hide-and-seek.

Mangos dance in the breeze, their laughter so sweet,
While turtles are practicing fancy quick feet.
The sun sets low, painting clouds with delight,
As all join the fun—what a marvelous sight!

So grab a drink, toast to the funny parade,
At the edge of the shore, where memories are made.
The waves carry chuckles, and the night sings along,
In a world filled with joy, where nothing feels wrong.

Chants of the Colorful Birds

Singing on branches, the finches take flight,
In feathers of pink, they dance in delight.
A cockatoo croons, with charm and with flair,
While pigeons play poker, not a worry, not a care.

Canaries in tutus put on a show,
While a parakeet juggles—look at him go!
A woodpecker knocks, with a beat quite absurd,
Providing the rhythm for all of the birds.

The magpies crack jokes, but only they laugh,
As the eagles soar high, looking down on the craft.
A hummingbird zooms, like a bee in a race,
And tips his tiny hat to all in the place.

At sunset they gather, a colorful mob,
With wings spreading wide, they've formed a great blob.
With laughter resounding, they take to the sky,
'This party is ours!' the birds all cry.

Tales from the Sapphire Waves

In deep sapphire waters where fish love to play,
A turtle tells tales that brighten the day.
Octopuses giggle with soft, squidly glee,
While starfish give thumbs up, 'This party's for free!'

A dolphin jumps high, with a splash and a laugh,
While jellyfish swirl in a giddy dance half.
They compete in a race—who's fastest of all?
But the sea cucumbers can't move, poor them, they just stall!

Coral reefs glow with stories untold,
As shrimp dressed in pearls prance, feeling quite bold.
A seahorse cracks jokes, with a flick of its tail,
And a clam chimes in, with a shell that won't fail.

With bubbles as confetti, the laughs float around,
Every creature dives deep, where joy can be found.
As the tides tell their tales, in the cool ocean breeze,
Life under the waves, is a party with ease!

Whispers Beneath the Palms

A parrot yells a joke so loud,
The monkeys snicker in a crowd.
A coconut drops with a thunk and roll,
While crabs dance on the sandy shoal.

The lizard in shades struts with flair,
Winks at the tourists, unaware.
A toucan's beak is a sight to see,
"Who needs a cocktail? I'm fancy-free!"

A sloth that naps through the sunny day,
Dreams of salsa, come what may.
The turtle chuckles, taking it slow,
"Keep up, my friend, you've got to go!"

Beneath the palms, it's all in good cheer,
With a sprinkle of laughter and a twist of beer.
The breeze carries giggles, wild and free,
Adventure awaits, come climb a tree!

Shadows of a Sun-Kissed Isle

A crabs' conga line grabs a glance,
While pelicans try their silly dance.
The sun reflects on the ocean blue,
"Watch me, folks, I can belly flop too!"

The seagulls squawk with comic flair,
"Hey, beachgoers, don't forget your hair!"
Sandcastles rise, but then they disband,
As an eager wave comes to make a stand.

A tortoise laughs, "I'm not in a race!"
As fast little fish zoom past with grace.
The sun slips down with a wink sublime,
"Remember darling, I'm always in time!"

In twilight's glow, the laughter begins,
A limbo line forms; let's see who wins!
As shadows stretch and merge with the tide,
On this isle of fun, let joy be our guide!

Rhythms of the Rainforest

In the foliage, drums start to beat,
While frogs in shades tap dancing on feet.
A jaguar grins, "What's the mood today?"
"Rhythm's alive—let's dance, hooray!"

The toucans hop, with feathers so bright,
While sloths move slow, "We'll join you tonight!"
A monkey slips, does a backward flip,
"Ooops! Guess my dance card took a dip!"

A waterfall giggles, splashing in cheer,
"Bring a guitar, a maraca, my dear!"
The vines sway gently, keeping the beat,
As creatures unite for a joyous retreat.

"To the grove!" calls the parrot with might,
"Let's boogie until the stars shine bright!"
The rhythm continues, wild and untamed,
In the heart of the green, every soul is named!

Serenade of the Coastal Breeze

On the shore, the breeze sings a tune,
While shells gather round for a picnic at noon.
Starfish argue on who's the best catch—
Suddenly, a seagull swoops in to snatch!

"Hey, you there, with the sandy toes,
We'll take a selfie! Strike a pose!"
The ocean waves clap, creating a show,
As dolphins jump high, putting on fo'.

"Who's got sunscreen? We're roasting like toast!"
A clam replies, "I'll avoid that coast!"
Laughter erupts like the bubbles at sea,
"Last one in is a rotten sea flea!"

The sun dips low, wearing a cap of gold,
The day's shenanigans, forever retold.
As night rolls in, we dance with glee,
To the serenade carried by the sea!

Silhouettes Against the Glittering Sea

Lounge chairs lean like sleepy sloths,
Caught in a sunbeam's gentle froth.
Seashells gossip on the shore,
While seagulls plot a snack galore.

Coconuts bob like lazy boats,
As tourists float in frilly coats.
Laughter spills from sandy toes,
While a crab struts, a dance it shows.

Umbrellas bloom like flowers bright,
Reflections dance in golden light.
Chasing waves, they start to race,
But oh! That splash, what a wet face!

Sunset paints the sky with flair,
Cocktails clink; do we have a care?
As laughter rings from this sunny spree,
We'll carve our names in sand, you and me.

Mysteries of Flora and Fauna

In jungles dense, the monkeys tease,
Swinging high with expert ease.
Parrots squawk, their colors bright,
While flowers bloom with pure delight.

Giant leaves like umbrellas wide,
Hide the mischief of a lizard's slide.
While bees dance in a busy buzz,
A frog croaks out, "What's all the fuss?"

Cacti wear hats of flowers grand,
Sipping dew, they just can't stand.
Tropical fruits, so juicy and round,
Roll away; it's a merry-go-round!

A leaf might fall from its lofty place,
Tickling toes in a gentle race.
With giggles shared in the insect's shade,
You can't help but join this wild parade!

The Stillness of Untamed Beauty

In quiet bays, the world stands still,
A turtle snores, what a peaceful thrill!
Palm trees sway, with a gentle caw,
As crabs enact their clownish law.

The breeze whispers sweet, yet slips away,
Tickling leaves in a playful display.
Daisies dance with a cheeky twirl,
While fish plot mischief in a watery whirl.

A sly iguana strikes a pose,
While tourists snap pics of their toes.
Nature giggles at the human race,
As sand flies up in a jubilant chase.

Even stillness can't contain the fun,
With critters laughing beneath the sun.
As shadows stretch, the day draws near,
We'll toast to nature, and to good cheer!

Prayers of the Sun-drenched Sands

Footprints lead like a trail of crumbs,
To where the surf meets joyous hums.
Beach balls bounce with silly flair,
While sunhats float through salty air.

Bikini tops, a fashion show,
As sandcastles rise, and flags do blow.
A flip-flop flies; it's caught in flight,
What's that? A seagull? Quite a sight!

The sun dips low, turning gold to hue,
Cocktails shake, with umbrellas too.
As laughter swirls in the dusky glow,
We'll let our worries drift like a slow canoe.

Prayers rise from the sun-kissed sand,
For more fun times, oh isn't it grand?
Together we'll weave good times anew,
With spirit, laughter, and maybe a shoe!

Conversations with the Stars

At night they blink, a silly chat,
'Hey, did you see that moonlit cat?'
They giggle soft, a cosmic joke,
'Watch out for aliens, they might choke!'

A comet zooms, a shooting star,
'Telescopes should strut, they came too far!'
Twirling galaxies do a spin,
'Is that a dance, or just the wind?'

A deep sigh from the Milky Way,
'Who left the fridge door open, hey?'
Stars trade secrets, just for laughs,
And send a wink to land's green grass.

In these heights, the humor's vast,
A starry night, a cosmic blast!

The Feel of Sunkissed Earth

The soil laughs beneath my feet,
'I'm not mud, I'm a ticklish treat!'
Sunshine rolls, a golden race,
With ants that march, a tiny chase.

Grass blades giggle, whisper low,
'Watch your step, you're too slow!'
A worm pops out, a comedy skit,
'Just digging here, don't throw a fit!'

Flowers wink, a colorful bunch,
'We bloom best when we have lunch!'
Bees buzz loud, they play their tune,
'Bring honey home, or we'll still swoon!'

Warmth surrounds, the world's a play,
Where nature jokes the livelong day!

Vibrations Under the Shade

Under leaves, a zany tune,
Fruits conspire, they'll be ripe soon!
The breeze, a rascal, tries to tease,
And shakes the branches with perfect ease.

Lizards lounging, sunglasses on,
'Is that a bug, or just a con?'
Dance of shadows, a tap and swirl,
Life's a party, give it a whirl!

Coconuts fall with a comical thud,
'Maybe next time, try softer bud!'
A squirrel's prank, he steals a snack,
Then zooms away with an acrobatic knack.

Living shade, a quirky place,
Where laughter hides, and joys embrace!

Fritillaries Dancing on the Breeze

Fluttering wings, a lively crew,
'Can you believe the things we do?'
Fritillaries swirl, a dizzy dance,
With every turn, they take a chance.

The flowers giggle, colors bright,
'What's that smell? Oh, pure delight!'
Life is sweet, like nectar's thrill,
'Let's sip and twirl, we've time to kill!'

Bees join in with a buzzing song,
'Fly fast, you can't go wrong!'
With every gust, the world spins round,
Joyful chaos is what we've found.

In this realm, with laughter spry,
Fritillaries fly, oh my, oh my!

Enchantment in the Canopy

In the leafy heights where monkeys swing,
A parrot shouts, 'What a glorious thing!'
With every laugh, they turn and dance,
While toucans gossip, lost in a trance.

The sloths hang low, taking their naps,
While iguanas strut in fancy caps.
An antlered deer raises a brow,
In this cool jungle, it's a funny show.

Frogs in bright colors jump and croak,
Joking around like a silly folk.
With a splash, they plunge in a stream,
Creating ripples in a watery dream.

Oh, the whimsy trapped in this lush place,
Where laughter's a currency, time leaves no trace.
A dance of shadows, a mischievous play,
In the sunny canopy, jokes will sway.

Trills of the Tropical Dawn

When the sun peeks through with a pinkish hue,
The herons pose like they just knew.
A rooster's crow, it's quite a sight,
Dancing flamenco in morning light.

Butterflies flutter, their wings a ballet,
While a cat meets a parrot, both in dismay.
'What's this?' says the cat, 'You've got no fur!'
The parrot laughs back, 'And I'm quite the blur!'

A monkey with style, a hat in hand,
Cracks jokes with the magpies—oh, isn't it grand!
As the sun climbs high, the laughter runs,
In the dawn's embrace, the fun never shuns.

The jungle giggles as creatures collide,
In this vibrant morn, there's nothing to hide.
A melody danced on the dew-kissed ground,
As giggles and chuckles in harmony sound.

Chronicles of the Drawn-out Night

As the stars twinkle bright over leafy beds,
Creatures gather 'round, sharing droll threads.
A nightingale croaks, attempting to sing,
While crickets chime in, modeling bling.

The raccoon's mask gives a quirky flair,
As he mimics the glow worms with flair.
A firefly buzzes, 'Check out my glow!'
But stumbles and lands in a loud 'whoa!'

An owl give a hoot, it's quite the jest,
As squirrels droll on who runs the nest.
They argue and giggle in starry delight,
Tales of the forest unfold through the night.

Bats do the mamba with such fun finesse,
While sleepy crocodiles lie back to rest.
These chronicles weave in the velvety shade,
With laughter and wonder, the night parade.

The Whispering Tides

The waves come rolling with cheerful sighs,
As crabs in tuxedos strut by in disguise.
A jellyfish giggles and floats with glee,
Saying, 'Come join the dance, it's all free!'

Seagulls squawk tales of fishy delight,
While splashes and laughter blend in the night.
A dolphin dives deep, with a wink and a flip,
'Can you keep up, or will you just trip?'

The sand tickles toes as the tide draws back,
While starfish debate their sartorial lack.
A clam tells a joke, but no one can hear,
As shells whisper softly, holding their cheer.

In the moonlight's embrace, the shore comes alive,
Laughing and playing, the night does thrive.
On this bustling beach, where fun takes a ride,
Such warmth in the waves, with joy as our guide.

www.ingramcontent.com/pod-product-compliance
Lightning Source LLC
Chambersburg PA
CBHW072222070526
44585CB00015B/1451